THE SLEEPY LITTLE STONE

WRITTEN BY COURTNEY LANDIN
ILLUSTRATED BY YANDEH SALLAH

Author: Courtney Landin
Graphic Design: Katarina Lapidoth
Illustrations: Yandeh Sallah
Editing: Taylor Landin and Daniel Landin

The Sleepy Little Stone/Courtney Landin
ISBN 978-91-519-8573-2
First Edition

Note to the parents:

This story is written to help your child learn how to relax their body and get ready to fall asleep. It's important that your child can learn how to relax and fall asleep without needing extra help because this allows them to fall back to sleep if they wake up at night. It is normal for a child to wake at night and it's healthy for them to know to fall back to sleep when this occurs. Before you begin using this story, read the section in the back pages of the book called *Happy Sleep Tips* and learn how to set your child up for sleep success.

Read this story in a slow, quiet, and calm way to promote sleep. You might feel silly at first reading like you are talking to them in this type of a voice, but this promotes a relaxation response in the body. Talk quietly and slowly, while stopping to take deep breaths throughout the book. If you choose, after a day or two once you know the story, you can turn off the lights and tell the story to your child, and let them relax while they listen. 

You'll see in the book, "pause, deep breath in and out." This is where you will pause and take a breath in and out. You can either ask your child to do it with you or you can do it on your own. If you do it on your own, notice if your child also does it!

Whether reading the book or reciting it, begin by saying, "Now it's time to get ready for sleep. Take a deep, calming breath in, and breathe out slowly. Feel your body becoming heavy and relaxed in your bed. Let's read about the sleepy little stone."

Let's imagine that you are in a forest and you see a beautiful blue, calm lake. The lake is very still and not moving at all. There are green trees all around the lake, and the orange sun is setting, which means it is soon sleepy time.

Now, I'd like you to pretend that you are a beautiful, shiny stone laying in the sand by the blue lake. Stones are heavy, so think how heavy your little stone body feels on the sand. Can you feel your arms and legs getting heavy in the sand?

From the side of the lake, you can see some
of the other animals in the forest are also
getting ready for bed. You see the mama bird
putting her baby birds to sleep in their nest.
They tuck their tiny beaks into their feathers
and close their eyes.

The papa bunny is putting his baby bunnies to sleep in their tree hollow. Their fuzzy bunny bodies are curled up cozy and tight.

The fox mama and papa are putting their baby kits to sleep. Their long tails wrap around, and they cozy down in their warm, dark den.

You can see a little bear family walking home to their cozy cave after a long day in the forest. Everyone you can see is settling down for the night. You yawn as you see them all going to sleep.

Take in a deep breath in and breathe out.
Try to make your body feel heavy and
relaxed, like the heavy stone you are.

You can see a family walking around the lake on their way home to get ready for bed. There's a little girl who comes running over and sees you. She picks you up and thinks you are so shiny in the setting sunlight.

They have a dog and he comes running over and gives you a sniff with his fuzzy nose. It tickles your little stone body.

The little girl shows you to her parents and they agree that you are very beautiful. She would like to take you home, but her parents say that you will be happier staying at the lake with your stone friends. In fact, they say you would be happy to visit your other stone friends in the lake!

(pause, deep breath in and out)

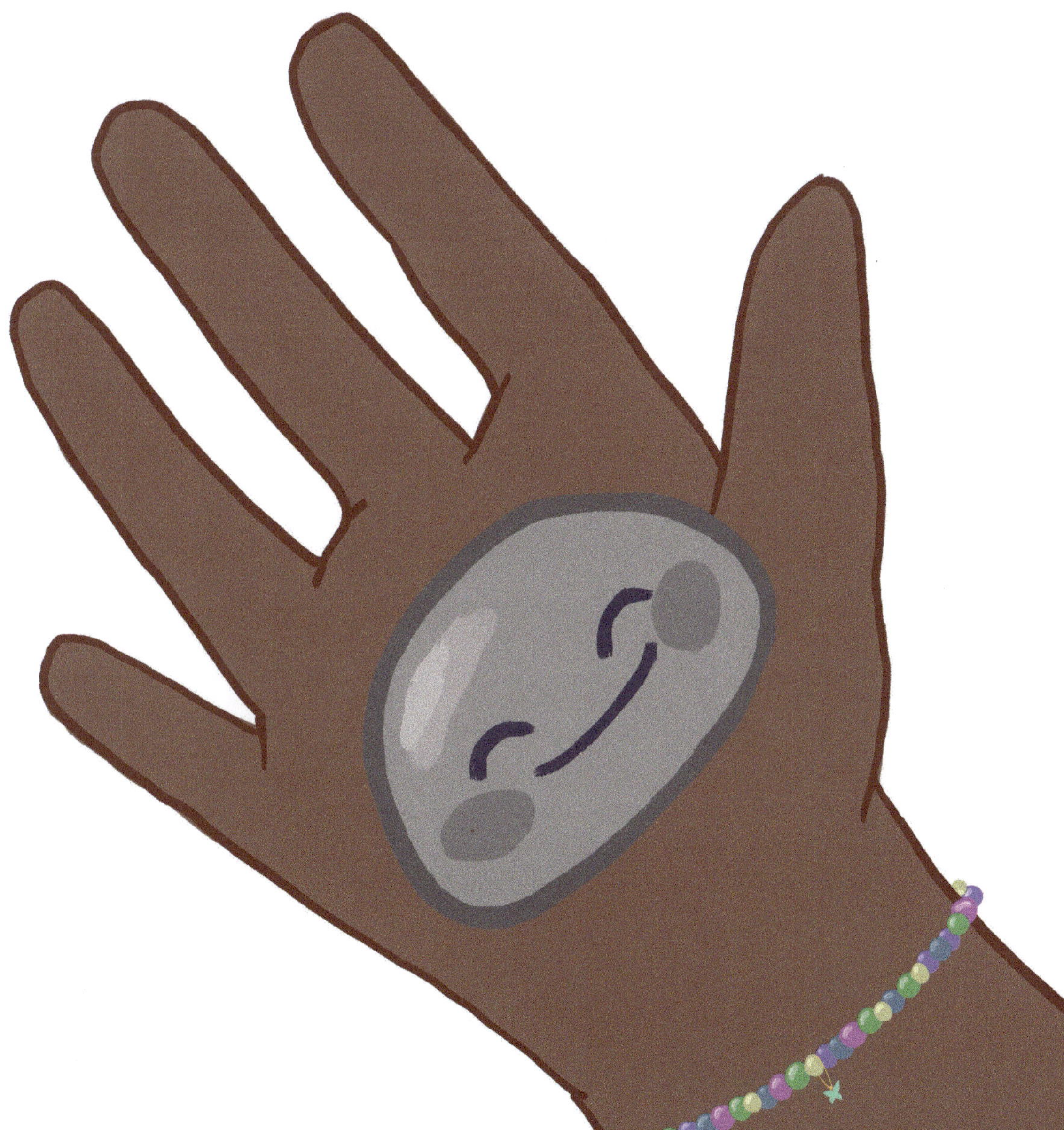

The little girl thinks that's a fun idea
and she tosses you up in the air towards
the lake. You feel light as you go up
into the air. You soon start going down
towards the lake since your stone body
is so heavy.

You dive into the water, and it feels cool
and calm around your body. Luckily, you
are a stone and stones can see and breathe
underwater!

(pause, deep breath in and out)

You begin to sink down into the calm, clear water, and you sway side to side as you sink down, down, down. It feels relaxing to drift side to side as your heavy body floats down into the lake. Feel yourself floating down side to side, like you are on a swing.

You can see everything under the water! You can see fish swimming by as they head home to go to sleep. They say 'goodnight and see you tomorrow' as they swim by you.

(pause, deep breath in and out)

Your little stone body feels heavier
and heavier as it sinks down into the
lake. Take a deep breath in and relax
your body even more.

You can feel how heavy your body
is as you go down into the lake. You
reach the sandy bottom of the lake,
and the sand feels cozy and calm as it
surrounds your stone body. You relax
even deeper into the soft sand.

You take in a slow, deep breath and you
relax even more after your journey. There
are other sleepy stones in the sand around
you too and they say "Goodnight and see
you in the morning."

Your sleepy body is drifting off
to sleep after your long journey.
Goodnight, my sleepy little stone.

Happy Sleep Tips

Falling asleep is more than just reading a story to your child. You must help prepare their body for sleep so that the combination of a bedtime routine, room environment, and a relaxing story helps them fall asleep and stay asleep.

Setting up for sleep

A consistent routine is an important cue for your child's body to help them know that sleep is coming soon. It helps to prepare the body and mind for sleep. Be sure to limit the amount of time your child spends on a screen before bedtime and set up a consistent bedtime routine.

Eliminate screen time

Screens include televisions, phones, tablets, and e-readers! If watching a screen is part of your child's bedtime routine, adjust the time when they are allowed to watch a show, and then replace the time at bedtime with a book! Any type of blue-light will delay the release or production of melatonin (the sleep hormone) and make it that much harder to sleep. A minimum of one hour without any screens is best before bedtime.

Setting up the room environment

Make sure your child's room is set up for sleep. We sleep best when the room is:

DARK – so dark, in fact, that you can't see your own hand in front of your face! Use blackout curtains or double up your curtains to block out any light from outside. If this isn't possible, make the room as dark as you can.

COOL – 16 to 20 degrees Celsius / 65 to 72 degrees Fahrenheit or cooler depending on the season. Our body temperature drops before falling asleep and this helps set the stage for our bodies.

QUIET – a quiet room is the best sleep environment. White noise is a great way to have the room quiet. White noise is a dull sound that helps drown out any other noises and cheap fans actually work great because of the dull sound they make and also keep the room cool.

SLEEPING BUDDY – your child may like a security item to help them sleep. A sleeping buddy is a great way to teach your child an important skill of self-soothing. This gives them a chance to learn how to help themselves when you may not be right there to help out. Make sure your child uses this every time they sleep but, don't use this as a toy. It should only be associated with sleep or comfort! You can use another comfort item (blanket or another stuffed animal, NOT a pacifier!) during the daytime or at daycare or pre-school, if allowed.

Setting up bedtime

Setting the right bedtime for your child's age will help their body develop a natural sleep/awake rhythm (circadian rhythm). An important aspect to this is having an early bedtime, because this will allow your child to get the right amount of hours of sleep at night. Don't think that an overtired child will sleep more and longer, in fact the opposite happens!

Children up to 2.5 years old do best with a bedtime around 7:00 to 7:30 pm. Children 3.5 up to 6 years old do best with a bedtime between 7:30 to 8:30 pm.

Along with setting up the right bed time for your child's age, it's also important to have a bedtime routine. This routine should be around 30 minutes and the same every night. This helps your child's body and brain transition into night time and also make a connection that this process means sleep is soon.

An example of a night time routine looks like this:

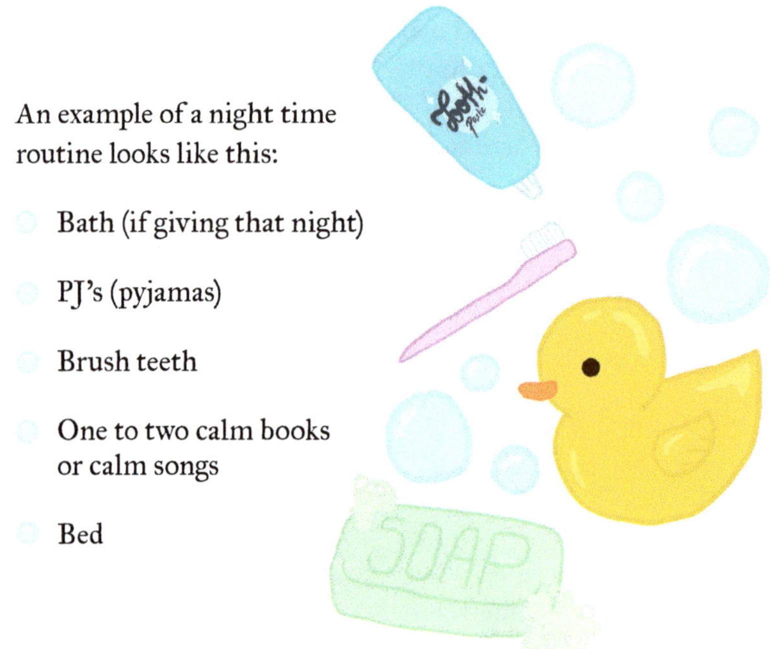

- Bath (if giving that night)

- PJ's (pyjamas)

- Brush teeth

- One to two calm books or calm songs

- Bed

BEDTIME ROUTINE
1 Bath
2 Pyjamas
3 Teeth
Story
4 Stories
5 Bed
click
6 Light's off
7 Goodnight!

Helping your child relax

Talk with your child about how their body feels. Ask them to feel how heavy their arms and legs feel in their bed. Can they make them feel even heavier? Have them take some slow, deep breaths to relax their body.

Read in a slow, quiet and calm way to promote sleep. You might feel silly at first reading like you are talking to them as if they were getting a massage, but this promotes a relaxation response in the body. Talk quietly and slowly, while stopping to take deep breaths throughout the book.

Do you know that it takes our bodies 10 – 15 minutes to fall to sleep and that is normal? So, it's ok if it takes your child 10 to 15 minutes after they lay down to fall asleep. This is healthy and in fact, if they fall asleep too quickly it may mean they are overtired and could possibly sleep worse at night. Allowing them to relax their bodies before falling asleep helps their overall quality of sleep, leading to a healthier child.

About the Author

Courtney Landin is a Family Health Coach focusing on exercise, nutrition, and sleep to help families thrive in this busy world. She created *The Sleepy Little Stone* to help her own daughter learn how to relax and fall asleep. It's still one of Taylor's favorite bedtime stories!

Sleep is one of the most important aspects for a family to thrive since it regulates mood, allows kids to grow and develop, learn, and also affects weight. If you are looking to make one improvement towards a healthier life, take a look at your sleep!

About the Illustrator

Yandeh Sallah is an illustrator and artist from Stockholm. Within her years of being self-taught, she likes to explore ways of showing emotion through her work, and in this book, taking a somewhat minimalistic approach to the illustrations.